OTH

C000257256

"Ed Luker's *Other Life* is a jewel box of scabrous pleasures. Ghosts, like debt-stricken poets, haunt bedrooms, underpasses and job centres. Luker's poetics of permanent crisis and contemporary absurdity invites us as howling accomplices." - Momtaza Mehri

"*Other Life* emerges from a dedication to poetry as a practice. Its 'Os' are as contingent and as potentially repetitive as the day itself is: spaces of pure possibility or a void where the memory of last night should be, self-exposing or else just exposed in apostrophes that don't so much appear in poems as surround themselves with the detritus of them. Composed or decomposed on the spot across 2016-2020, they register the highs and the tawdry political lows of that period through the totally circular and nevertheless essential activity of addressing ourselves to it, falling into holes, climbing out of them, making a mess of things, and trying again and again to bear one another up. From the 'smoked out intimacy factory', a cloud in trousers goes up in fitful plumes." - Danny Hayward

"This is an expulsive and generous book. It gives out, offers a place to see the night from, then comes back as expressive calls, nasty laughs, sighs, strike songs, kisses, 'red bull puss', lours and falls. The trajectory of poems is the seasons of the spirit, rhythms of rest, the calendar of action, outlines of wants to be out and in, in the aftermath of the body you take to the protest with you. The self is ironic but never dismissive of what can be and needs to be done. The political friendship of Luker's lyric voice laments and offers itself up, looking for things to be up for and how to push back. I love this book's edging of loaded and erotic adjacencies; 10 years since a riot, the night before the day, the toe next to the big toe… in undulating registers Luker bring poets voices back to us; Raworth tones, Mendelssohn chords, and then a clear voice talks to us with doubt, with care, with solidarity, in memory of hard defeats, shared, then reformed as plans, muscled in as desires." - Holly Pester

ISBN: 978-1-913642-29-7

Book designed by Aaron Kent

Edited by Aaron Kent

Broken Sleep Books (2020), Talgarreg, Wales

Contents

Other Life

Ed Luker

Aubade

for Tom Raworth

Split light, densely unequivocal
some sick in the cereal

puffy in the cot
fat in the artery

eyeless we bevel
our own extraction pads

against the spleens
strewn in the corridor

some would wish
for less all the time.

Moon Bathing (after a night walk)

Fucking hell,
did you
          see the moon
          last night?

Half asleep,
Andres
          knocked on
          my door.

We walked to
the marshes
with the dog
(named Luna)

                    bathing
                    in its blue

glowing ring

its big O, melancholy
on a stick in the sky.

Huge Moon

I can't
stop
thinking
about that
huge moon
morbid O

symptoms
littered
across
the sky

the air
stuffed,
a viral
ring or
crown,

O huge
moon
what is it
that you
want
from us?

Moon Poem

It is a drag
to tell your secrets
to the twilight hours
whispering close dream
and to have the moon
not let you go
to the land of sleep
            as it keeps,
weighted & luminous,
pressing on your eyelids
through the brick wall.
Is it strange to call
the moon luminous?
I mean, what else?
It is the moon afterall.
So I wake, little else to do,
with the real morning
with the actual morning of
the absolute sky,
and drag myself
into the crisp
(im)mutability
of a song lighted
in the next air
from a distant
bird's mouth.

How Did You Survive January?

How did you survive January?
I drank, and then I didn't.
I went to the gym a lot,
stopped going to the gym,
and then started again,
noticed every small declension
in the condition of the world,
logged it in an etching on brown leather
in pink crayon behind my eyelid:
from my abdomen,
to the cracks in the tarmac at the bus stop,
to the salvation leaflets, gambling forms,
and tax bills stapled on your forehead.
I ate healthily, concertedly, emphatically,
then didn't eat at all,
breathed the miraculous air and then spat it out,
terrified by the definite fact of reality continuing;
I would open the front door,
close it, open it, close it again,
then upon opening it,
I would prise through the gap this spinning disc,
this undulating, ululating,
beautiful peach cream of the pink sky,
this, the world still continuing
to be there, this
each time it swung on its hinges,
that's the this of the door in your face,
this certainty of going on, as the sun rises and slams
against the bonnet of the day's sick crest.
I washed my sheets a few times,
Roti Factory, next to the launderette,
changed its name to Roti Restaurant;
I don't know if it is more like a factory
or a restaurant but the roti is still good;
I stomped around outside
in the not cold enough cold

of our ecology collapsing in front of our eyes—
talked to friends
about our incessant hearts breaking—
it's like we have all internalised,
well, I wouldn't want to

the silent stupor
of endless brutality marches up
along the sidereal alleyway
of the burning phantasmal collapse
of continuous reality management,
the spinning digital pylons plaited
through the ricocheting satellite sky,
as the rats rush past

in a world where nobody gets what they want
except some people get fucking loads
of what they don't want
because they don't want anyone else to have it.
I would walk across the marshes at dusk stomping
through the intractable interiority of still being.

Yesterday it was thirteen degrees celsius,
in fucking January,
and yet I was still too cold,
revived myself with two hours at the Russian banya,
calmed by the fact that no one was talking politics,
in English at least.

January, a climactic slump, the deep freeze of a blue spirit
crushed in the antechamber
of this small island's pitiless cruelty.
I think of the white English taxi driver at the spa,
sat in his pants with his belly out, engrossed in a video
on a large screen of a man
playing Mozart on a piano to an elephant;
I think about how the elephant swayed
and we are supposed to think that this means it
enjoys the music but how would we know otherwise;
this morning, I fell into a pit of snakes, again;

I started counting all the utensils in the kitchen,
laid them all out in a long line, end to end,
starting with the knives, then the spoons, then the forks,
then moved on to the larger utensils,
the line started to snake around the kitchen,
down the corridor, past the bathroom,
to the front of the house,
and back again,
a domestic arabesque.

January? I left the house a few times,
in search of more utensils,
and then stayed at home.
Sometimes I checked my emails,
every now and then I would apply for a job,
every day I woke up and fell into the spike trap,
every day I awoke and tripped into the tar pit,
every day I arose and was arrested by the medieval police,
thrown from my bedroom into a dark basement,
from which I would clamber out every day and continue
on my merry seditious way;
I started to split the utensils in half, length-ways,
so that the line would reach further.
Eventually, I got a job.
From time to time I answered my calls,
then stopped answering my calls,
and then started again
(apart from unknown numbers because I am not ready to
die).

How did you survive January?
I chalked off the days on the wall
in the dark recesses of my medieval cell,
the days of January, 2nd, 3rd, 4th, 5th,
13th, 14th, 15th, 28th, 29th, 30th, 34th, 56th, 67th, 103rd,
nobody knew it had so many days,
just like nobody knew the tremors of fascism,
the propertied delirium and boredom
of Enfield, Woodford, and Harrow;
the screaming slammed door in your face is

the felt reality of this ideology,
of misery's endless sacrifice of joy
at the altar of mortgages, smoke alarms,
car loans, can openers, vicious racism,
class antagonism, screeching silence, monogamy,
the sheer fucking dull stupidity of the nuclear family.

In December a hefty blade nearly sliced one of Tom's fingers
clean off from his hand;
he was just trying to put a leaflet through a door in Canter-
bury
when his movements triggered an anti-burglary device;
everyone was white and miserable, full of resentment
but I don't think they should pay for healthcare.
The man trimming his hedge with a yellow convertible
in the driveway was unsurprisingly rude. Fuck Canterbury.
In Kensington people were either really rich or really poor,
with barely much in between,
apart from walls and security devices,
and all of them maddened by the fact
of being where they were.

I knocked on the door of a man on my list
in a post-war brutalist housing estate,
he was not the man named on the sheet,
still I asked him if he was going to vote,
he was a middle aged North African man
wearing an FC Barcelona shirt,
the television was blaring loudly in the background,
he said he loved Jeremy Corbyn but he could not vote,
I noticed that he was crying. When I left him,
I stood in the stairwell and cried.

How did you survive January?
I stopped reading the newspaper,
threw my laptop off the end of a pier,
gaffer-taped all the glass on the windows of the flat
in the hope that it'd stop them rattling in the wind,
spent several hours in 'downward dog',
started talking to the birds at the bottom of the garden,

started knocking on the doors of all the houses on the street,
said hello my name is Ed did you know that…
a few slammed doors in my face,
I would try to say hello my name is Ed did you know…
a few more slammed doors in my face…
I would try to say to the doors
on my street of my neighbour's face
hello my name is Ed did you know that
Boris Johnson is a cunt and Sean Bonney is dead.
The phone kept on ringing
for the unknown numbers,
I would sprint to the front door
and ask the nearest stranger in the street to answer,
they'd say yes we're sorry it's true
Boris Johnson is a cunt and Sean Bonney is dead;
I collected every drop of rain
for the whole month
in a cup on my windowsill,
decanting the water in the cup
into a larger trough just below.

It's over now and perhaps we can commend ourselves for
that,
if you are reading this then you aren't dead,
congratulations,
it was cold,
and yet it was not cold enough.
I don't know what to do next.

How did you survive January?
I wore your love bites under my t-shirt like a secret charm,
each toothmark a bruised letter of an unknown alphabet,
memory pressed into flesh.

I got mad,
I howled at the moon
like a sick dog.
I thought about my friends,
called them up and
we sat on the phone in silence.

The Human Body is at War with Itself

I am on the floor of the Buddhist centre,
don't ask why, I mean, really, I could explain but

lying in shavasana, I hear a police car outside,
mind wandering, I am asked to give heed to my breath.

There were days this summer where it was so hot that
everything stank of death and our throats were dirt.

And breathing in the moment of the blue siren scream
I wonder what hurts in this city where restraints never cease.

How many made homeless today by heavies and bailiffs,
how many lungs heave and anxious chests tighten because

the bills and debts pile up on the doormat,
unopened as fear grips the vertebrae all clenched.

London, where the bubbles swell and knives burst
and everything is indexed to its impossibility

for those without, and the price is the extension
of the dreams of all who profit from immiseration.

The city of sharp increases, we handle ourselves
against the calls and clamours to work for more.

The share price of Foxtons Group PLC was up this morning,
as Phil Collins sings another day in landlord paradise.

And this continual dispossession has its own order
of movement, as knuckles flex in eager cop gloves,

unfurling like a hibiscus flower in a glass of champagne,
each new day brings the working of the old laws.

Standing skyscraper tall, spine straight, capital sings
the body athletic – taut steel embraces pinnacled glass.

How many doors have the Met Police smashed in
across the last few weeks and how many young men

were arrested on suspicion of being little else but other
-wise indifferent? The violence of the demand

for transparency: put your thumbprint here.
Sit down. What did you say. This is very serious.

Anything you do say shivers down the traces of
your nerve-structure, as blood swells blue to the surface,

in the dark corners, away from the cameras, the silent treat-
ment,
confined impact, a jab, capillaries burst in this trauma.

You know and I know, it is as simple as this,
the human body is at war with itself.

Pouring One Out for the Petite-Bourgeoisie

At the Ledbury,
shards of a thousand years of compacted pressure,
borne of fire,
pierced through the taut surface of the camembert
with revolutionary exactitude.

Lissitzky with the crystalline edge
forced into a splintered baseball bat.
Pour one out for the petite-bourgeoisie,
a nightcap to end all nights.

Small business döners cleave the meat
from fresh importation of the Afghan poppy,
every scratch card and coke can on the Kingsland Rd
realised in human traffick.

Some of my friends are forced to sell their bodies,
I sold mine by choice,
                              lay in bed
for two weeks, read *Invocation* by Jo Walton
and
        watched *Transformers: Dark of the Moon.*
I hate Shia Laboeuf, every movement of his hideous face.
I wish Eric Cantona would drop kick it
into oblivion.

Back in East London
Cantona's fish chase the trawler,
transmute into an army of bipeds,
kill the crew, throw them overboard,
and commandeer the boat to Dalston.
assassinate every bearded poet.
Pour one out for the petite-bourgeoisie,
a nightcap to end all nights.

Scum is the by-product,
it drips from the pavement into the gutter
amassing in the vomit of every 'creative'.
It bleeds through the drains,
beneath the surface lies a secret history,
the weeping sore of bitumen
with its teeth ripped out
and red bull puss
an oleaginous mist of Unique Selling Points,
scum,

          as in, Looters ARE,

          as in, they scrape away and erase,

                    they continuously

   deface
the surface, a truly Euclidean plane.

Someone told me it is only realizable as an idea,
hammered into the terraform.
When I walk down Broadway Market,
I think about fire,
I think about police,
I think about the nightstick,
I think about how stupid fashion ninjas look,
I think "Why the fuck did I just spend
£3 on a sausage roll
and why does it come in a box?"
Pour one out for the petite-bourgeoisie,
a nightcap to end all nights.

The fish arrive from Dalston,
dragging the severed heads of poets by their beard hair,
some smashed up grit and washing powder
rubbed into the chin of the poet Iain Sinclair.

The voice of Iain Sinclair speaks to me,
he says "I am your father," he says
"so much talk about the underground is silly.
WHEN it would require a constant effort
to keep below the surface."
I stare into his beady eye:

"Hack…Rose…Red…", off with rose head.
His head in my hands,
I hold onto his ears,
the mouth still jerking.
Pour one out for the petite-bourgeoisie,
a nightcap to end all nights.

The lights go out,
his eyes go out,
two pearl earrings roll from
under his tongue.
I pick up the dead head
of Iain Sinclair.
It is now robotic & cut
from circuit boards
of Rwandan coltan
stitched into the collective memory
of the AQA assessment team.

Dropkicking the android head of robot Iain Sinclair,
I scream fuck the surface, fuck my AO2's,
fuck staying above ground,
if I mean it – it's only when I pay it
                          and the underground road
was real. In Paris, Beckett fled the Gestapo
and Alfred Peron was captured.
The shopkeepers
wanted the state of violence
to secure their profits.
They wanted scum
swept away, to disappear,
the state can make you disappear,
one cannot refuse.

In plain sight,
so off I go to Ur-Bane Outfitters,
to clothe my crushed soul in the darkness,
pour one out for the petite-bourgeoisie,
a nightcap to end all nights.

I reach for my balaclava
Nathaniel Turner had visions
of blood on the corn,
the first shall be last,
I shall be somewhere,
in a library, writing a poem,
the quaint ink
of my quill
caressing the parchment
with a quickening fervour.

How is class constituted
in the concrete lobster pot
of post-industry, how do
its conflicts appear,
who and how many will die,
what songs will we sing
to remember them?

after staff chased off the looters,
guests were given glasses of alcohol
including, champagne and whisky
to calm their nerves

pour one out,
pour one out,
pour one out.

On Yoga

On the way to the yoga class I am wondering whether I should be attending said class at all | I can feel this semi-anxious urgency thrusting itself out of my chest | It's the sort of energy that I sometimes resolve by getting really drunk | We all know | Because we have all been told | Many times over | That binge drinking is bad for you | Bad. For. You. | Bad for you | And then, when you try and not do the things that are bad for you | Invariably, you find yourself doing the sort of awful things that make you feel like A Good Person | And who the fuck, may I ask, wants to be that? | So, it starts with a little yoga and | I imagine | It ends wearing a loin cloth polishing a small black pebble with a brush with three clusters of hairs for fourteen hours a day in a wooden hut somewhere | Anyway, yoga, yes yoga | It's good for you isn't it | Good people do it | I arrive early because I got the time wrong | So I sit outside the centre in the small garden with all the other burnout people in recovery anxiously clasping at their enamel mugs of green tea | Knitwear everywhere | I'm early and I already feel like I don't want to be here | I go down into the yoga basement | I know it well | When I close my eyes I know what size and shape the room is | I can always place myself within this room | I lie there and take a meditative pose on the floor | My knees are facing upward | This allows my back to be flat against the solid ground | At rest | My eyes are closed | Open | I am trying to clear my mind of thoughts | Closed | Trying to clear my mind of thoughts | Trying to clear | My mind | Now Open | Trying clear | Clear | Neural Flash Trap | My mind | Carpal bow string eye | Gouge neoprene tongue split | Of thoughts | Anyway, I know the room | On my back | Breathing in slowly | Breathing out slowly | I know that I feel more relaxed here | Count the seconds between each movement | There is space here | Open your breath into the space | Feel the slow expansion and contraction of your ribcage | The spaces in between feel more porous | The lesson hasn't even started | This is just my internal voice talking me through my own pre-class relaxation | Feeling | Things | Space| Emptiness | Clarity | Tibia xylophone | Refracted through miasmatic trowel | The class starts | We are asked at the beginning if we are in an energetic mood or a subdued mood | I am the only student out of about sixteen people to put my hand up for energetic mood | Having been mostly at home all week applying for jobs I do not want | After a couple of weeks of applying for jobs I do sort of want with no success, so far at least | This is the chest energy | The thrusting out | So, yes, it will be a relaxation class | No sun salutations today | Time to relax | The yogi encourages us toward stillness | Enwrapped by the silence of being | We are invited to draw our mental attention to the smallest parts of the body | In sequence | Place your attention on your big toe | Give your mind to the toe next to your big toe | We dwell on each element like this for a few breaths |After each toe it is the entirety of the foot | Next, the shin | Subsequently, the thigh | Then, the entirety of the whole right leg | I must be honest, this does not come naturally to me | Patience | What else? | After five minutes of intensified focus on each leg | The mind lingering within the cells | Blood and vitality drain and fill like large sacks of dog vomit | Eventually we have covered the entirety of body with some sort of intense focus | I do not trust this | I do not trust this, I do not trust this | Everybody loves the sun, sure, sure, ok | I don't doubt that | But I do not love everyone | Anyway, my mind starts to cleave in two | I shit you not | I see across my mind's eye this steel edge | Like a knife carved a slit into the night's canvas | On one side of this cleft everything is dark | On the other it's like all of the mental energy of *the entire shit* starts oozing out | What is that mind | It breathes ghosts and molecules through the neon dust | There's this halogen lava lamp exploding in my frontal cortex | I honestly cannot hold onto that kind of light | It corrodes something | The weight of the dead | The sheer presence of history | Some kind of trip | Open | Close | Breathe in | Breathe out | Unclench your heart | Mine is trapped and ripped up inside yours | And bad breathing is a kind of habit of the hostage situation | Anxiety pangs and pins cells to dust | Waste burdens under human fret | These manifestations of human happiness in deep set focus | Dreams unleashed from within the inner state | The cut in the actual sky | As sheer relief is trepanned in like bombs from a phosphorus engine | The hole that we tore in the fabric of space time | I wouldn't do that if I were you | I leave, quickly | Awkward smiles | I watch the crackheads on Roman Road struggle to pick cigarettes out the gaps between the slabs | What does presence give to misery that misery doesn't already know for itself.

Fun Fair

O! heavens to these
immaculate hells,
between all this,
the ears, the light
fails, grey matter,
thud. Fucksake.

It is too hot
do we live to dream,
we do, of
each caress,
fractured
this holding all
or spin out
in endless stupid, stupid
the sushi belt at the end
of the klaxon, klaxon!
At the end, choose best
wisely, new friend. Yours.
Insert two fucking pounds.

The alarms ring out
ever new emergencies of,
oh shit, what is this crisis, again,
I have lost my place,
among the pretty angels and sexy devils
of this dead set wreckage,
the gap between
necessity and finitude,
shit in a bowl,
poetry,
microplastics,
fire in the augury,
carousels of giant clowns,
in the guts of Love,
wrestling the radioactive

octopod army in the green sewer,
the Slush Puppy dog
floating upstream to Valhalla.

But we get used to it,
we do get used to it, we do,
feeding our demon pets
horsemeat in the iron barns
on the squatted Soviet air bases,
feeding our familiars
the nucleus of dead stars
behind the funfair
of insidious desire
behind the backs of our pitiless neighbours
who we spit at, in disgust.
Oh snort this with me, won't you?

I will die alone,
and you will die alone,
and mother gently weeps,
into a distant phone.

I stand atop the acropolis of piety and somehow
know myself to be better, as in *not like you* but
a *better person than you.*
I shout in your face to let you know this.
You don't look pleased.
But what do you know?
This will be good for you.
Everyone has their price.

Poetry has wet hair
if you brush it
it falls out

you have to taper it
back,
it's like that, sometimes.
Rip it from the roots.

It is cruel to keep going
over the lines,
start
again.

Strike

It is late, I am at home,
I am late to rise, having felt the fall
what is the shape of the question?
I was never great at physics
but the first step is to draw the line
you stand behind it
it is late, time to get it
cos it's out we've gotta go
and as a geometry the picket

> is a line
> and a breaking
> of lines

what does that mean:
it means shout the fuck up
and move.

Palace Secure

Palace secure
exit door
walk the street
kiss the feet

rain falls
fire rises
centres fold
pets: prizes

May comes
May goes
winter waits
heaven snows

tables spin
hedges trim
assets grin
futures dim

blues blue
skies melt
stable true
pain felt

oh carousel
oh fixed abode
calamity
down the road.

For Dich

To you, my ghost, whose movement a breath that animates the air. There's another side of hell. The only clanking chains the ones overburdened by association. The tongue furs its own dust, adequating particulars to the unparticular. Exeunt. Pink rusts its day a high on close bordering a sun melting into the acrid sky. Enter. Exeunt. Enter. To you, my my, whose memory clings around all edges. Several species of larger mammals still exist by the Pripyat River. They are indifferent to the end of history, indifferent to the end of the end of history, which is yet to feel like any kind of beginning we want to be in. To you, my ghost, an entanglement of particles at the level of this transfer, a lapsed time, the only continuities in germination. All our philosophies attend to smithereens. Never at rest, only an eye bent on continual vacancy. The lost lot of love's rot, garments gangrene garlands gnashing at the smoked out intimacy factory. Für Dich, *Unterm Rand des ersten Blaus.* And how it steals all away as we scream into the air, the corporations of ourselves and others. The localised anxiety of bodies soaked in creatine and ecstasy. I only count losses in petals, I only count petals in salt, I only count salt in sequins, I only count sequins in moons. Are the ghosts the skin and film that cover the rot of our wounds? Once in a blue boo to bosom the bud of collapsed *oiko* oink assertions in geo gear of soft power. Every border to life is shrieking against its wreckage. To gaily fade and sit amongst the absence. *Exeunt, damnit exeunt!* Shepherds seeking angels on wet and windy payday. Oil baron owns yacht to staunch the hole in his leaky heart all tied up with love, broken branch, broken gossamer, broke for busted gums and over the drifted cascade of smidgen pink that spears the cosmos inside out. To you, my ghost, a memory of germs – *spit, sniff and shiver*. Sunrise and sunset in the aging romp of the arms racing around the burning pandect: to live and shuck oysters in Hiroshima. Go past life, go funereal disco floor, go trounced shells of effluvia, go two sticks tied to the underpass. But leads nowhere. To you, my ghost, I give this, a cascade of wires wrapped around the trunk of a tree. Ditch your drenched out palms somewhere to kiss the sky again. These compressed separations of production that interweave back in the dead lands. The polythene pressed against the cold lips, unmoving. A basalt rock flips into unmarked waters. The movement of the dead persists under the lids of expectation. Our understanding of geological time is premised on continuation but what if everything had stopped moving already and was rather merely being dragged around. The tongue laments its own wagging split of serrated catachresis addressing my molten vacant briar on the coursing song of harmonic incompletion to the ears of razor capstans in eternity's secondhand bargain graveyard.

My Ghost

To you, my ghost, a gift. In ceremony the wrench of pinched harmonics at the angelic entrance of downward play. Pinhead pining in dirt to russet opacity. Each petal a ploy to pay for time's spectacular demands. An array of missives in the degraded key. To you, my louse, my wretching invertebrate locked to a husk of wheat that I call a memory, a membrane, a meteor, a mite mighty *mine* me my measure that I deign to call an absence, split between the neuro-transit of skin's slick persistence to the surface of the corporeal: a true blue negative that we call a phantasm. Photo-*genesis*: carry all your dead thoughts around in a wheelbarrow until the axle grinds through its own weighted dismay, its shrieking rotation aiming at the angelic order. Winter itself, is filled with you; the streets that dip then rot with the embittered frost of the future's persistence, still tapered to an itch of the past in its pressing dread. The branches are in a conspiracy, slowly secreting their wish. The germinal bursts rupture through a granite bolster. To you, my my, a phantasm grown out of that building there, that being there; that tender loosing of tilling to the wave of working out and back through it, the past to which the mind runs continually toward. For the birds, for the birch barking back being bitumen between biting breaking beat beat to beneath or ne'er. To you, my hands outstretched and open for embrace, dirt under every fingernail. O outgrowth of persistence, O vine and root of impervious disregard for catastrophe, O natural ignorance, for a few threads of your perpetual maneuvers outside of the constancy of loss; would I were too undressed from this.

Bad Day

Ah,
good old
bad day.

Poem

The unfurling assonance
of verbiage,
impossible solace
in the age of
tender gardening,
trowel furrows
a knot wedded
fingers in disarray
we clamour pains
don't open I want
you just   on hold
a fire licking the
edges of foreclosure.

Poem

It is warm on the porch.
The sun sets, and I,
having little else,
an addiction to
intensity, a spark thrown
out, denying its own,
imagine a desire
scatter it around.
O words,
is that to be, a man
these garlands of feelings, thought Vesuvius,
but rather more a belch.
Small birds
fly out our wounds.

Poem

Readily, to will to unfreeze the blood
        I set myself a side and lay next to it
sleeping in somewhat of a ditch full of shit and potpourri
        smell the drains
and the requisite legwork
of crawling up the leaky pipe of the heart
burdened by a fantasy that begets itself.

Poem

I am out of love with time
its joints lay heavily on mine,
there are threads, bows, stitches
that carry it
straining at the seams,
when they swing
which way
            do they break?

Poem

When I die bury me beneath
the chancel of our hearts' most blistering speech
and for all occasions we shall use the napkin rings
no longer eating the sinews of elk served on a platter
masked by the torn leaves from the annals of 1493
so shall in first light each star prick the colander's dementia
when I die bury me gently
each handful of dirt
so left unsaid there is much that burns in its flight
tearing through this land of no refuge compacted into a
sheer example
and on who's hill shall we stand and watch the drowning
and titter disapprovingly on such unpleasant ground
that it stop us from falling is sure proof enough
of what we risk in song
but you are sickened by this address
a paling art.

Poem

Vichyssoise and halibut switch for the liver sausage
sandwich they jam up their advances and playing it
by suppressing death in Frankness to claim him enthusiastic
where the enormous history of American death is just a trivial
inconvenience like the indifference to whether you get paid on time.

You await the pay off. I feel it there too, even though I am not American
and O Amy Winehouse we are you, which might be part of the problem,
the proliferation of symptoms in address playing out to the fanfare
of the french horn in the next alley-way in which we are not standing.

And the problem is less changing the guard or their socks than friends
on benefits or friends who can't get benefits or how identification
secures the exclusion of those who aren't friends from the conditions
of survival. I want you to tell me it will get continually better forever
or it will get so bad that it must get better eventually because at the point
at which it is interminably bad people will decide that at breaking
they won't want to die — a fantasy of coherence and to hell with it
as the experience of suffering is anacoluthon, what we are yet
I know not. How you go next I know not.

Back on My Bullshit

I will do it tomorrow,
today is Tuesday,
yesterday, I am indifferent to it,
but *Vorrei spiegarvi*
Oh dio, rosso, blau, schmeckt,
the edges of memory
tatter this skin
we feign to live within.

I will do it tomorrow,
snogs in the key of life,
this is my comeback album,
let me explain, oh god,
I have drunk all the wine,
indifference won't kill you,
and neither will wine,
do not speak of it, love.

I will do it tomorrow,
that will be Wednesday,
I am over today, please
come down. Back on
my bullshit, why don't
you stop, listen, stop, no,
don't, I can't, it's diffic-
Oh god, let me explain.

A Nasty Poem

Poems are nasty, or
pouring yazoo up your wazoo
      a flaming phlegmatic turd in a bow tie
stick my spleen back in with the lid pierced
you are never going to happen guess what
      next month is a leap year
hic rhodus hiccup hick
      panky out my shoehorn
don't act like you don't always know what
        I am thinking
he says let's rest in the shade
on the plains of Calabria the wages are marginal
there's a petrol pump leveraging your eyebrow, topical
      to the chorus of tears
an inflated skip full of pesto and a bargain bucket
are a canvas for class antagonism on the walls
of some sort of community funded regeneration Twister
      so the intern sticks his left hand up there
and the Free Gift was product displacement, surprisingly
a giant blue circle of unhappiness, how does that
      make your feelings known
chose to buy a forkful of antihistamines with some curtain
      hooks on them
this is your best moment as a reader
you've gone radge in a duck pond
      dry eyes and shitty breath.
This is the conclusion, after a cream horn at the bus stop.

Clown Town III

Poems are so embarrassing, or,
when you have no money
dress your little lambs as gremlins
and take them to the Job Centre
to get fake gremlin jobs,
not meant for lambs.
And the muse says:
get your shit out my fucking business buddyyyy,
then your fake gremlin lambs will
have fake gremlin lamb babies
and you can cream off their wages and benefits,
the milk & honey of the DWP.

It's like being stuck with your bad thoughts,
plucking a lone lyre
sticking your head in a fire
eating marshmallows out your arsehole
inscribed on a big stick
that it keeps bashing you with
in public, like
oh there's my bad thoughts again.

I am the poetry boss
because I am embarrassing
I am the embarrassing mob boss
of poetry, gorging myself to death
at that nice restaurant atop
the peak of Mount Parnassus,
on that fancy expensive food £££
cooked angel livers and devil's gold
and I can't even read the menu
because it's in Ancient Greek.

I keep clicking my fingers at all the waiters
their cloven hooves clop-clopping
cussing me out in Ancient Greek,

I point at the menu:
"I'll have some more of that, errmmm,
how do you say 'poetic inspiration', please."

Like, so I took you to Clown Town,
and I was incredibly excited to take you there.
I even wrote about it in my diary. But
I had a bad dream returning, an anxiety dream,
a dream in which I was very, very anxious,
where I was crying in the crystal shop.
I don't know why, I just started crying
and then I couldn't stop. You laughed at me.

It's the matter that keeps dragging you back thru hell,
So, I took you to Clown Town and I did cry,
in the crystal shop, the shop with the crystals, and I put it in
                                                    a poem.

It's the matter that keeps dragging you back thru hell.

That's Us

after Arthur Russell

that's what I mean
something about that address
is always the signification
of an absent temporality
it is the before we got there of some
sort of having with you
troubling the circulation of all this bad air
built on the motive working against us
and you are not even here to listen
as I am not yet capable of being

                        the one
who speaks the words that sustain
our communion

              but possibility runs
across veins like the constant transformation
of matter into something other than the object

that the bare fact of life shrieks out
across all borders to it
and that is pop's greatest lesson
that the instant gratified presents the phantasm
of some sort of universal joy
that it will never let you have
and continually works to suspend
the radiant glimmer of its dispersal

       hangs in that suspension

but sometimes you just look out the window
and it's full of cops
that's no lie

Break Poem

and it is recursive this
line snatched from what we can
make of it a promise to
bear our burdens together by
throwing them upwards where
the sex of this is getting turned
from within so without
and in that sense, this is where
eros gets in as all the demands
of our thinking of our being
must urge towards that and its
limit of being turned inside out
where to break is to wrest away
whilst holding those who are too
broken   and as Jasmine says:
how do you cross the threshold
of that fire, of that burning moment
in the anticipation of being hurt
where what you most want is to
end the conditions that hurt you
your friends
                    but eros is war's
weapon, force means violation
as an open secret of territory & property
how do you expropriate those
for whom that continual violence is glee
is the fucked affirmation lingering in their pay packet
where the very possibility of these people being
made anew seems to bang your forehead through
a piece of continually shattering plate-glass,
                                        our
thinking is recursive because that is the
turning and breaking of the copula
a duress that wills to be snatched back
as you and I cling to it,
                    nails break in flesh

Poetry's Non-sense

Poetry's non-
sense is that it is not
music's non- sense, which
is in the blood, diffuse,

but poetry is the heart full of
that blood and looking to sequester
it
   to get it held there and fixed
where the music flows out
and circulates back round
the beat of each
                one

how to break poetry
with music's generosity
its indifference to players
such that all sense is social
because the sight is in kind
and not some crosshair of new
markets, or some locket of
the poet's hair pressed in
the hand of those who do
not want it,
            all locked
on to some particular
who is possibly only
looking to evade this
                death

Love Poem

O! To be in it so in it that throughout
the curvature of the body each of each
cell trembles within an immaculate breath.
Dirtied fingers pulse their own tips,
sweet to lack these unsavoury thoughts
slip through the trellis of palms, arms,
necks and unassailable dreams of
momentary happiness, fragmentary
air of that snatched and stolen,
dig the thrown irreverent garden,
ciphered ink of the pang scratch,
return trinket of criminal excess,
fictive granted to the bound
less limits so love's law the transgress,
hot buttock in pinker truck,
in love's work the genitive oblates
that this particular reinscribes,
as the capture of fantasy's own
demarcation of property rites.
I've been half in love with love,
tethered to half this death
but every possession is marked
by its own undoing, this giving
without being given that within
we stand in love to fall so trying
to fall whilst slipping not to stand.
The complications of having and giving
of being had to the given:
love's gerundial at the interim of ethics
& the *imago*, we capture our best
for the worst, trying to untie the making
of better from the forbidden, so biding,
a tryst in neuter of the fantasy of genitalia,
a currency of bitter failure and damage,
it's the idea of the you that must breach
to you through what it makes in the I,

if everyone in the world could give me
what I wanted, I would no longer be
that pitted against the every one, so nulled,
the ligative loosens against the tightening,
so refuse cuffing against yr wish,
in sprung the new season now
throw all the jailor's keys in the lake,
dream to breach the dream's versus
of un-conditioning the conditional
so excess as a stem of what is (im)possible,
now flowered so crushed to real
and burst open the cell walls against
this auto-immunology of common feeling.

No Eden

after Les Guérillères

the possible world is a garden of
impossible speech
                    new names for each
some spread out on commons
of melons and paw paws
fresh in flesh and pith the produce
of life in common words
without toil

to till our tender hearts
afflictions into   this
new briskness of abandon

when we down tools we down tools
and caress each other's foreheads
licking the sweaty brows
unburdened to new natures
cross-pollinated spirit
laid out flat amongst ice's lack

as the garden floats into the drift
a beaten track, a no-go zone this
blistering heat rupturing the terraform

Song for No One in Particular

I am starting from the question,
are the intellectuals the enemy, of
some possibility of commonness, against
their best wishes

how do you get them to throw down
pulled away from the pit of thought's
production, into the dance

heal yourself and move, or
move to break your self
the same proposition

and what some commons means is, O
       you are stoic in the face of isolation
and loneliness is not universal
but constituted by its diffusion
marking the spaces between,
             the temporary break out
which you felt as the tonal rupture
but we stand on our word together
with the word being the communion
and there is lack where we look for it
as the lines move to demarcate loss
getting thrown around like a dance
joy to stand against the lack there is
which we incessantly will to find
mastering the pen for our soft fingered prisons

       that's how it works out
so many false hoods to try on
where the dress up is always disregarded
as surface play, yet how do you get to wear
down this life of the wronged round the best
way back to the way out from which you start from
distinction and our common touch

both abraded by the stolen life
wishing to sequester yourself behind all those books
we wrack our knuckles on your door and ask you to

    get down

In a Blue Dream

the blues, after Tinashe & Ian Svenonious

in a blue dream
                         is the party the site of refusal
what we owe is (in) this breach of the favour
where I may not remove
            in the mutual render
                                    when I said
pour one out
                  for the phantasm of the enemy
I arrived at the wrong party

for the inhale
should be the expectancy
of some new stars

            what is the exilic but presence
            the first work of mourning
            is the righteous refusal of rights
            for the lament is incantatory

            pour it free
            things get
            turned outward
            because we
            pull them so

                  how do I get there
                  on my ones

you bring the outside in
by breaking the code

                  a ten step program
            it starts with
                  a broken ankle in
            the mouths of the wronged

and holding this breaking inheritance
of the hold together
something bruised like
the hickey underworld
what we owe
this breach of the favour

Under Lied

at the footfall of a mountain of suffering you
                    found yourself
              with me

in this consideration of what
              attention
                          might aspire
              beyond,
the fixing encoded through
                          co-ordinates of woe,
demarcated by possession as a force

                    of carbine rifles,
                    of razor wire, o,
                    of the whole spectrum
                    of psychic torture

and again, you (don't want to) remember
          the breezes back, again
              the rains back again

          sodden season again,
          the flakes fall,

you walk across
              the open hearth
                          in the moment
                                    of recall,
dressed to meet
                    the eve
              but still
                          bathed by the touch of winter
                    sun's
          last light,

balanced by the distance of heat's tempo-
ral
spin,
note how much
bleached, by the recent
the feeling of catastrophe,
at the edge of your tread the land weighted

innocent lack,

fantasy: the known
grief strewn across the top
soil,

as sure the eye does come
to pass on some
verdure

aspect
ready in waiting   to be cropped
by the seasonal blades, or,
picked
by the working hands of labour's bidding,
pressed
into gangs housed in the cradle of oversized
anderson shelters

of spirit's nostalgia for its own extinction. do not cry,
for the heroes do not enter here, a fiction they do not lie in
wait for this
is an announcement that their recovery is a
saline
solution.
the same said for heroines, each to their
owned
fate. their warrant voided. when permit-
ted

you will come back

getting past the perimeter fence,
you reach the check point

the human cosmos   starts fitting
the blood into its type.
                      the welkin sets itself up
to take stock of retinal alignment,

            each distant glimmer refracts
            through the vitals of our inward

                              throes,

the border guard stares stiff at your replication,
in that moment of transport, passage granted, to explain
your
self to fate's guardians in an identification of the terminal

in that you know, this
                      is the shore of the world's
                                    total hori-

                      zon

past the gates, you skirt across the perimeter of the city's
edge,
the limits of the acceptable polis
                              are at your touch and
in this moment the recall
                      is to the idea of what the city
            means

at the known touch of its exterior
                              what borders
to the city,
            amongst the many cruelties
            the winds
blown, waves
            higher than the scene of remembrance,
            so much the time has passed, but amongst

the granular surface
                    underfoot you can still map each of the lost
in the place that they finally came
                        to be understood as gone,
or where they arrived as complete
                        cherished by disregard

            after all elapsed,
            after each of the
            bodies had been
            counted
            and weighed,
            such that loss
            was known
            in its exactitude,

                        but the bodies had not been
                        entirely lost, for they were
                        so upon their arrival,
                        being from somewhere
                        else. these cities had been
                        intensifying
                        for several years,

each inhabitant wondered what weight they could

bear,
you knew that no good would come of it
        this hard edge of the nation,

                            softened by each last
                    spray
of the cold surf flecked
                    across your cheek
                                    exacts
a micro pressure,
                    the insatiable hunger
                    of oceans of grief,
                    in graft the night

blurs for the descent, your feet clenched in the bed
of the foreshore begging the sea to part,

      yet you
           plead to the star
that the mythos of safe passage
                  be built
      from the mouths of innocents,
           in their speech, as each
      fresh crash mounts
           its sorrow to
      be sewn in the scree
           and at that edge the vision
      could from this be
           built a limit
      as the constant amongst
           the endless heat of
      outgrowth carboniferous at the brim
           of cumulus and the city scape,

what is it from
     this most imagined depth
                that draws its extract,

      mined deeply,
           the contours of the soul,
      the pneumatism of the mind's
           eye can drill for sediment
      is there to be burst through
           the crux of embedded hope,
      in this graphic vision is
           the tangibility of imagination's
      entanglement with power

                in dreaming, matter does not stop

                   where the total miasma
                   of a national capital
                   demands it to, biometers

                              plugged in the stumps
                              of blackened plexiglass
                              fractured and burnt
                              by the secret police
                              of the plasma soul
                              that won't let you give
                              up so easily

so echoes strain // our possible intimacy

that we had most known how to traverse each trap
before it sprung
                              where the anklet wraps around
the solitary
                    the contours in isolation,

                    in some impossible
                    dimension we had
                    tried to imagine
                    the establishment of
                    a mode of non
                    -being from
                    which flourish
                    would not be
                    put to the anvil
                    of
                       their fabrications,
                    would not be
                    pressed into their
                    velvet palms slickened
                    by the quick pressure
                                        waves,

their seismographic presence floating its stock
in the roots of the somatism
                              of each heart's garden,
the cavernous balance of each
                              needle tracing its weight

across the aperture, felled on a slight premise,
of for whom
        the felled storks
     dropped birth // drones
     caught
        the products of love
        in giant nets woven from the
disused electrical cables
            harvested
                from outmoded techne,
tend to the ruptured wing of the stork

                as it was
the motion by which our orders of the revolutionary as
conduct itself,
      tattooed in microscopic lettering on the
      spinal ligaments of the newborn,
how else to avoid the
        tortures of the state's agents
for what, the sacrifice
        of those craning wings lit up
        by the weight of secrecy
dragging the promise of some yet unknown engagement

what for it
      but to shoot our flaming arrows over enemy

lines snag the barbs caught between the babes' teeth,
as the drones harvest their helix-datum matched
        against
the projections our enemy tied to the yet uncoded trivia
    of daily lists of arrests
        and incarcerations predicated
      through predilection for the phrenic,

           for the admonishment

of those already destitute to stay so

as the non-factual

cosmos wills it so in its mythographic charting,

    in its flighted contagion,
    that it be willed by their morn and
    calmed by their eve,

        as the stars turn through their owned

          motion,
            beaming the infographic
          treatise of
        whichever

       hell
         they own

           and wish
       for the profits of
        to unceasingly

            extend

in aeons of atomic light
    emitted at scales known
only to those for whom
    the law is most balanced
that it re-
    sets the curse of diurnal
tread as if the grains of
    sand could compress in
to a wondrous patience
    wrought by crystals
emerging as cabbages
    in the jeweled sill-boxes
of the inner
    city apartments
of those
    professionals
who will always

know that their sun
sets with the gain
of a glimmer and
rises with the
joyous breath
of being right
where they want
to be known
as lawmakers
for all future,

                puppeteers of
                fortune, cartographers of
                the condensed markets,
                a yet reached milky way,
                professional disregarders of
                the outperformed
                galaxies,

whose light lagging in non-unity compounds

into a refracted stellar dust.

On Defeat

What does it mean to feel like you had your moment,
that time is something that has been stolen away from you,
that in the aftermath of that theft I a moment I your life is now
no more than the expenditure of compressed air leaking out
the backdoor, out a hole bored through the permafrost
stuffed down to the bottom of the planetary movements
of the universal dirge of the tepidly incinerating binbag?
Not that the moment was just yours but that its possibility
had been snatched away from you as the lid of the horizon
slammed shut on your fingers strapped to the underside of
the chassis of failure, irreverent chariot, because you then
were not you, not in the way that you feel yourself to be now,
how long can we mourn, endlessly diving into the river,
fiftful, broken and tired I exhausted, empty and spent,
and that is what movement meant, to have been thrown, wrenched,
taken up: to have had every sense that possibility itself
had come truly alive with the future's promise of its own end,
the cessation of the pressure of the measure of days,
a ring of batons, a chorus of orders, a phalanx of shields,
digital clocks falling out the sky, every second suspended
in the instant of its trembling, a giant hourglass spinning
round as the riotous dissolution of time as it is felt when it
breaks you, fireworks racing down the throats of policemen,
paint flying across the windows of every store on Oxford Street,
marching past the Ritz, hungering to eat their opulence,
marbles under the feet of their horses, hideous horses,
past all the monuments to vain glory (masking death and sugar),
as truncheons cracked skulls, as sticks flew, as it all burst out,
that you found yourself hurtling towards a sky on fire,
with the joy diffuse in communion, as a condition of trust,
blessed to be taken apart, tender and ready with your comrades,
movement itself a taking of parts. And what has been stolen,
sequestered into the cells of the regular clipping of the imagination?
Now all feels withheld like a swollen door ajar in a damp flat,
where nothing lights the spirit because the isolated cold
fills our every breath with its rot. All this stale air,

all this time compressed in our shoulders. And, friends,
it is rotten, to have had history pull you up and spit you
out again, for a few good moments, for nothing more
than debt and waged servitude, all the hours stolen for gas bills,
their world not built for you, its monstrous incursions
of spectacular boredom, the sheer misery of getting by,
the mob's grief with a pang, and now without a mob.
And the pangs ring harder as our bones chill, waiting,
we drink til dawn and hope to find something in it,
this city is full of wolves where nothing is plenty for them to eat,
they pull apart the sinews of matter, on which we expend
ourselves paid down in rent and double rent. It is
the exhaustion, a cloth pressed firmly round the escape pipe,
troubled air smothering and poisonous, nausea & inertia,
as smoke fills your tear ducts and the tongue dusts,
two twins holding each of your hands and nailing you
to the floor. And what way to get out when the escape is full
of rats and the hatches are being smoked out
with putrescent black smoke, all the exits bolted shut.
I'll be honest I want to shake you out of this,
I have wanted to for quite some time, it's been too long,
I want to pull you out of this wretched hole, I can't grasp
how you're so gripped by this, it's been far too long.
And I speak through the imperfect medium of you,
for your moment, because they are my moments, too,
all of the moments stretched and then compressed,
into the edge of the present and held against our throats.
And I never really understood why people would want
to set all of the institutions on fire, apart from prisons,
but now I'm not so sure, burn it all perhaps.
I didn't want to set the academy on fire, I wanted
to take it apart very slowly, brick by brick,
with all my friends talking and smiling as we lay waste –
book by book – to the academy,
mapping out the stars of the negative,
such that our moment would not be explosion
but the turning inside out of the present,
pulled through the restitution of everything
pressed up against itself, implosive sparking,
like unwelding the seams of the world's currency,
such that the stars all shimmer, red and tremblant,

and the world's two faces collapse,
the sky tinged pink,
with the promise of possibility.
But now the tigers of wrath
lie sedate in their cages,
and the whispers of fire,
burnt out, we're dormant,
with you I want to imagine
a place where this
is not enough.

Poem

Under a bower
      the head rests on moist earth
  wetted folds in the neck evading sky
      light flashes through blades
the blaze of warming heat in haze
     a jubilancy, a shimmer,
      a tremblant stress
of this rest drawn from the fresh dawn
as the sounds of words prick the ear
    the clearing of light
     pulled from the din.

Poem

Ruminant,
      in the midday sun,
merrily I squander myself
    drunk on borrowed time
as sheets of pollen lodge
    in nostrils and on tips
across planes of separate interest
       the twitch and sniffle
           of seasonal joy
each sneezes their own regard.

Poem

At the close

       of the day

  numbers

      fall

  from the sky

  exit currency.

Burning a decimal point

  through the solid earth.

You know this

     have seen it

  sinkholes

     thirty feet deep.

What we call collapse.

Poem

This ground beneath us
shifts in its constant,
as we traverse the rise and fall
calling out the names

for those who have escaped us.

We bring our flesh to our memories
press our memories into flesh,
tied to a tiring expenditure
but still, effervescent in the crest of life.

It's the curvature of this skin
lost again in that slippage,
a heart's flutter at finger tips
a tripping spectral flash within.

Fierce Unbearable Summer Part II

Hot like fire, like each flame a lick of entropy,
as the impossible heat death of carbon pressed
into the absent tonsil. There are teeth in Every
Thing. Under the tongues there are more tongues.
under those tongues there are even more tongues,
except they are cold. Too rotten to flicker, or
fling any sound aside from this doubt and out
under the piles.

                         In this dream I was being
chased by the ghosts of soldiers, except they
were only just dead, nearly alive. Everything was
on fire, absolutely everywhere. Exits all shut.
The intimation of the humanity of inhumanity,
what we call the monsterous, which is always
the violence that cannot be understood.
That there are people and they will kill you.
The floorboards were flagrant beneath our feet,
falling down, into the infinite chasm of absence.

          Now in the sun
          I am impossibly eager for everything,
          not death.
          and O!
          How through the shine
          after all life
          the spirit is in heavenly ascencion,

like rice pudding spilt down your shirt at the after party.
Like lobster meat hammered into the keyhole
of a police cell, like all of our hopes laminated
around the edge of an infinitely slamming door.
And we fight to steal ourselves away from sleep,
towards something not shit I dedicate all the
fantasies that aren't mine or could have been
mine, hardly, like fill all my cavities up with

whipped cream, drain all the moats and wear
crocodile boots on each of your ten toes
to the job interview where you will always
be naked and slowly someone starts to flay
your flesh with a stanley knife sharpened
on your baby molars. In the interview they
start to ask you a riddle. It is premised on
translating the language of the sun into
an Ancient Indo-European script, at the
point at which you start to understand what
the task is the cleaner asks you to leave,
except you did not know that this was a
space from which presence could be
evactuated. You open the bolt hole with
your elbows and attempt to step out, it
involves a movement less like out and more
like up but also simultaneously down.
The cleaner has started to pour a highly
flammable gas everywhere, coating every
surface of your internal memory. Even the
rice pudding starts to smell like flambéed
lobster meat eviscerated in the core of the
furthest star of an unknown constellation.
At the point at which the rice pudding starts
to seep into the squamous disintegration
of every hot idea of self-presence that
your integration of thought and action
can muster that you log off and say,

     FUCK THIS.

Spring Chicken

Six wings &
a can of 7up.
I am sunk
drunk
in the depths of rent,
stumbling across
the Kingsland Rd.

I breathe and live
for debt and bills,
all between
is hot gas of dumb experience,
you fucking moron.

Property is the most cherished virtue,
clipping in a world of hyper-speculation.
my soul drenched in neon bin juice
stapled to the creperie for £600000.
your digital canvas of louche non-expression
on display at all hours.

How are we caressed? Is it a constant delirium?
The lines run away, endless, each tangent
an interest for all those who hold all
bestow it for their blessings.

I am everything my student debt does,
folded into slushed collateral:
the drainage runs deep with blood
the riverbanks of electric currency.
work work work work work
and whatever else there is.

Touch the outer world's data shop.
it is a sweating greasy brow,
making bread for crumbs.

more life built into shadows,
other than this life,
the most certain path.

I guess that's that.

On Debt

What is it, this oblivion?
The explosive edge of spirit furled
out at the dawn chorus
that we carry inside us?
What I mean is, what is this trapped nerve?
Trapped in the gut, trapped in hunger,
trapped in rot, so trapped in the
everything that we are ever not?

Inward hope an imploded stop,
a node of joy reversed rewrought,
forward to what could a reroute
work in joy to sing throughout.

What do we know about each other?
I know that I wake up with an
irrepressible hunger that has turned itself
inside out. This feeling is destitution,
in standing alone, I split to a constant fall.
I know that I feel my heart in my chest
pinnacled to all debts outstanding.
Tell me all about you though…

Everything we've ever had and now all
at once, everything pressed into this black hole.
And what is dark matter
but the revenge of dead labour?

I heard that you have a lot of potential.
I heard that you have a lot of potential.
And sometimes we like to think of catastrophe
as the great leveler, like "Fuck it,
how much can I loose from zero?"
Well, how much? When being pushed
down, perhaps we have to remind ourselves
that those with the most to lose will do everything

they can to ensure that you do. Lose, that is.

I find it hard to be sure about much,
in this, I am sure:
I don't want you to get crushed.

Heart Strokes

I

O, sleep,
I don't know her,
I writhe around the marsh lands
to the heartbeat's
anxious arrhythmia,
the trombone solo of the pineal gland
in the dewy dawn,
the heat,
an intensifier

I have fucked it
the idea's arrival
jumping a gun
the crisp shedding of leaves
my naked shame
trees spit the silver tears,
entrails and roadkill,
I listen to the best of The Prodigy
taking wonder in the star-studded streetlight,
an ecstatic preludium to failing better,
in the heat's
desire

this tar and feather engagement
I call out to love
under the morning's moon
of not knowing,
of hurting
again,
effusive the
bitten rain failing against
the hot tar
a wet heart
doused by

itself, when
every
thing
is on
fire,
again.

II

O, world, sorrowed sore
what thought bears out, I weep
to let it go

the sun
so hot
as heads rise
a new day phase,

what death clings
to feeling,
to knowing,
tremor and palpitation

I keep that
good good, heavy goods
in my head today
the weight of the world
a slick wrestling disaster

one thousand million gallons
of crude rushing through
the aorta, blood in the guts

in every heart a forest fire,
in every heart a bad desire.

O, my mouth opens
with the smoke,
saying fuck it,
have I fucked it?

III

O, heartbreak, peaking, returning
in the time of peak oil,
every barrel is less a decimal than
an explosion underneath
the lake of life itself
that slicks into the soul,
vomit
beneath
a zero

why walk
when you can run
backwards

crash into the pit
of spikes
again and again

love among
the terror
of comets,
still,
the fires
burn.

Joy Again

To my accomplices,
O, of the possible,
I sing in kind:

which is to say I sing pushed up against a limit
point to be live within the line of all pressing forth
and perhaps joy is the delusion of the line break
-ing of things to break from without or within
and so flames do as in possession they rupture
in body of boy break in as that spark to not
be: to out the I together and this stand from
which the flex of muscle the stance to break
out with joy in flame now together is pressed
again, pressed against the necessity of dis-
avowal of a blunted spirit, to live in the balance
of account, singing from without in the count
all the properties spilling out from the rim
expand the limit in a slackening so sing to
stretching where we are as a rather not be-
yond in outgrowth of self-floresce to make
the un- in habitable a scion of the new and break
       each determinant of property's speculation
       which is to say so sing pushed up against
       now in seize delimit

       this point

to where the body is lost in its song
how in character as the transmitting it
could break forth as a possible we
such where we singing we are is breaking out
we are the throat's stricture is of person-hood
in the history of mass is damage seized,
lend and borrow, we break and burn, they bury
so take back everything they have stolen
so to mourn the loss of everyone

O lives grown new in the re-entered garden
to the we planting against this theft
not civic: all love brings damage over
breaks the bounds of being in *polis*
an incriminating   (of)   possession
what does love break out of, so how
does it restore that which must be broken
such are the stakes that we might inhabit
a break from that which we no longer
can be in but must live through so out
but joy bounds the not of what we can't be

Acknowledgements

The poems in this book were written across 2016 and 2020. In order of appearance, iterations of many of them were published, in print and online, in *The Fanzine* with thanks to Aurelia Guo; *HOAX Magazine* with thanks to Lulu Nunn; *Roti: a post-election reader* with thanks to Mathura Umachandran and Orlando Reade; *Prelude Magazine* with thanks to Stu Watson; *Poetry Review* with thanks to Mary Jean Chan and Will Harris; *Cumulus Journal* with thanks to Katy Lewis Hood and Dom Hale; 'Fur Dich' and 'My Ghost' were collaborative responses to artworks and images by the artist Alice Morey, created for an exhibition 'never, never, ghosts' at Rosina Studios, London in January 2018; eleven of the poems were first collected in a chapbook called *Compound Out The Fractured World,* released in a print run of eighty on RIVET. Press in October 2017; *Queen Mob's Tea House* with thanks to Cornelia Barber; *Summat 4* with thanks to Alex Marsh and Tom Crompton; *Salvage Magazine* with thanks to Caitlin Doherty; and, *Blackbox Manifold* with thanks to Alex Houen. I want to finish with an expression of gratitude to Aaron Kent and Broken Sleep Books for publishing this work.

LAY OUT YOUR UNREST

Lightning Source UK Ltd.
Milton Keynes UK
UKHW020736040121
376189UK00004B/62